MARIA MAR

or

the murder in the red barn

MARIA MARTEN

or
the murder
in the red barn

A Victorian Melodrama

EDITED
WITH AN INTRODUCTION BY
MONTAGU SLATER

HEINEMANN EDUCATIONAL BOOKS
LONDON

Heinemann Educational Books Ltd
LONDON EDINBURGH MELBOURNE AUCKLAND TORONTO
HONG KONG SINGAPORE KUALA LUMPUR NEW DELHI
NAIROBI JOHANNESBURG LUSAKA IBADAN
KINGSTON

ISBN 0 435 23810 8

This version first published 1928
New material © Heinemann Educational
Books Ltd 1971
First published in this edition 1971
Reprinted 1973, 1974, 1977

Published by
Heinemann Educational Books Ltd
48 Charles Street, London W1X 8AH
Printed Offset Litho and bound in Great Britain by
Cox & Wyman Ltd, London, Fakenham and Reading

CONTENTS

INTRODUCTION

The first known performance of *Maria Marten* was at the Marylebone Theatre on 6 April 1840, although there were probably versions before then. The play is perhaps the most famous of all the melodramas written for the popular theatres of London between 1780 and 1850.

William Corder actually did murder Maria Marten on 18 May 1827, just as the play relates, and a pamphlet describing the trial sold over a million copies. *The Times* gave six columns, or a quarter of its entire space, to the report of the trial. Corder's defence was that when – as the play tells – Maria, disguised as a man, met him at the Red Barn, she shot herself, whereupon he in panic buried the body. He went to London and advertised in the newspapers for a wife, had forty-five applicants and married one of them, a respectable school-mistress. In 1828, after Mrs Marten's three visions, the barn was searched and the body found; William was arrested and, on 18 August, hanged before an audience of 10,000 people, who afterwards filed in slow procession before his naked body laid out in state in the court house of Bury St Edmunds. There, his skeleton is still preserved along with an account of the trial bound in his own skin. The rope with which he was hanged was sold at £1 an inch. He has had the honour of being included in the Dictionary of National Biography.

The minister of Ebenezer Chapel, Shadwell, London, went to Polestead and preached an open-air sermon near the Red Barn on Sunday 17 August, 1828. In his discourse, 'which was intended to alarm more than comfort' and which has since been published, he said: 'From what I can gather from the best sources of information, fornication called, and justly called, in the Prayer Book of the Church of England, deadly sin, is increasing among the poor in the villages of our country, and I fear that events in this neighbourhood establish the fact. O young females,' he continued earnestly, 'time was that your mothers and grandmothers possessed almost so much chastity as the middling or the higher ranks of society!' He was, no doubt, referring to the fact that the Maria of history was not quite the heroine the play would suggest. She had already had two illegitimate children when William met her.

The play had its greatest success in the provinces. Portable theatres and barnstormers spread Maria's story, and in a sense the version used in this edition is a barnstormer's version. It was written by John Latimer, writer in ordinary to the Queen's Theatre, Battersea; John Latimer's son ran a portable theatre and carried the version about the country, and it was his step-son who made the manuscript available for publication.

The manuscript was written in an old exercise book in scrawling illiterate handwriting. Spelling and punctuation had a marked individuality. Stage directions were indicated by hieroglyphics which have been translated and to some extent expanded. In the present version the punctuation has also been slightly modified.

Like all melodramas, this one is full of echoes and half-remembered hints from a score of other plays. Writing a play was considered to be an exercise in patchwork, and it is impossible to say where all the patches first came from. Actors who knew and frequently played after a fashion a dozen Shakespearean parts lapsed occasionally into blank verse and unquoted quotations. The gipsies who wander without warning into this play were a convention in Victorian melodramas. It was felt that their presence brought a touch of poetry. The 'pull London, pull pudding' scene also occurs in other plays.

Victorian Melodrama and its origins

Maria Marten is only one of many highly popular melodramatic heroines. They were all seduced – Agnes Primrose, Lucy Lisle, Zella Lee – the catalogue could be extended indefinitely, and they all came to a bad end. Yet they are all heroines. It is a large family and not so old as one might imagine; investigation leads inevitably to the conclusion that the family of seducers and seduced had its origin at about the same time as Wordsworth.

In eighteenth-century literature, seduction was not practised on a large scale. Johnson in his Dictionary seems scarcely to recognize the proper meaning of the word. One of the most popular novels of the age, Richardson's Pamela, had a heroine who was always on the brink of ruin, and the daughter of the Vicar of Wakefield actually fell. But between these ladies and the Maria Marten sisterhood there are some important differences. Goldsmith's heroine, Pamela, insisted on a certain minimum of formality, and would allow herself to be deceived by nothing less elaborate than a mock marriage. Pamela too, in spite of great provocation, did remain technically pure while Maria and her sorry sisters (though it would be a crime to doubt their essential spiritual purity) definitely did not.

The curious change in social habits which produced in France the guillotine was responsible in England for the Romantic Revolution. After that revolution the distinction between Soul and Body was firmly established: common-sense and sharpness of intellect were recognized as despicable when compared with nobility of soul. It was by this means that Seduction became for the dramatist a workable theme. It was now for the first time possible for a heroine to be innocent as to soul and experienced as to body; to be imbecile and yet to be adored.

The first great pioneer in the struggle, in so far as it concerns the stage, was a German dramatist named Augustus Ferdinand Freidrich von Kotzebue. He wrote the first play in which outraged husband and erring wife are brought together by the tender prattle of their child. *The Stranger, or Misanthropy and Repentance*, as his play was called, was in its day immensely popular and translated into every European language, including Greek. The main point is that the heroine, Eulalia, really had been guilty. It required a certain courage in a writer to give her this latitude in a serious, not to say sentimental, play. He succeeded in shocking his first English translator, who went to the trouble of remodelling the play and undoing the deed. 'He has not made the wife actually commit the crime which is a stain to the female character,' he says, apologizing for himself in the preface. 'This last liberty (he trusts) will be excused; partly because he feels that, according to the dictates of nature, reconciliation would in such cases be more easily obtained, but chiefly because he considers it as more consistent with the moral sentiments and more congenial to the heart of an English audience than the forgiveness of a wife who was actually guilty.' This was in 1798.

This squeamishness disappeared in later translation, and from that time one may safely say that the English branch of the Marten family was founded. From now guilt, if anything, improved a heroine.

There is a theory that the inner meaning of all these seductions is found in a sort of class war. In the eighteenth century the average London theatre audience, consisting of Society in the boxes and the stalls, critics in the pit, and gentlemen's gentlemen – always more snobbish than their masters – in the gallery, would have had a certain fellow-feeling for the Seducer. They would have derived no good moral lesson from the play. But in the nineteenth century there appeared a popular theatre, in which heroines had a chance. It is recorded that, in the 1830s and '40s, whenever an aristocrat – that is an actor in a silk hat and gloves – appeared on the stage of the City of London, Whitechapel Road, or the Pavilion Theatre, Mile End, there was immediately a howl. There was no choice but to make him the villain. And probably this spirit of class helps to explain the unnatural power with which the villain was at first endowed in the difficult art of seduction. He had an odd capability of going the whole hog without any help from the lady. But when the period of the decadence of melodrama begins, and we come to the time when plays are written once more in the West End for export to the East End, instead of the other way round, the villain takes to commerce, is liable to be Jewish and has no supernatural powers at all. He has to buy his prey.

Later versions of *Maria Marten*, written for portable theatres and provincial stock companies, tend to develop considerably an element which was latent in the original drama. The villain is given a new weapon: Maria falls to prevent an increase in her father's rent. The play then revolves round the ancient theme of 'The Price She Paid' – a theme Shakespeare embroidered in *Measure for Measure*.

The Victorian Theatre

Thus it was that the drama of simple seduction grew up, flourished for a time, and then silently disappeared. Melodrama belongs essentially to the period of stage history when the minor theatres of London were at the height of their power. They shaped it according to their own fashion, to suit their own needs; to understand it, it is necessary to understand them.

Whatever the cause, there grew up at the end of the eighteenth century, for the first time since the Elizabethan Age, a demand for a popular theatre. After 1780 there began to appear in different corners of London what one might call 'Theatres of the People'. They were illegal (for only the four patent theatres, Covent Garden, Drury Lane, His Majesty's and the Haymarket, were licensed to present stage plays); they were democratic; they were the oddest places imaginable. They posted themselves in the most distant corners of London, for there was need to de-centralize theatres in the days before buses and tubes. In a curiously contradictory fashion they were London theatres and provincial theatres at the same time. Each developed a style of drama suitable to its own district; thus in the two Whitechapel theatres it was usual to have a kindly old Jew in the play whenever possible. But in spite of superficial and local differences they were the same at heart. To a great extent they shared the same subject matter.

Soon every district had its theatre. The Surrey and the Coburg (afterwards the Old Vic) served Lambeth and Southwark; Sadler's Wells served Islington, Clerkenwell and the North; there was the Britannia at Hoxton, the Fitzroy (also known as the Queen's, the Princes', and the Dust-Hole) for Tottenham Court Road and Seven Dials. Besides the outlying minor theatres, when the demand for theatrical entertainment in the centre of London started to grow, two illegal theatres were opened there. Astley, the proprietor of the famous Circus on the Surrey side, bought an old French warship, the Ville de Paris, in 1805, when it was sold along with some other prize, and had it rebuilt more or less in its original shape – but upside down – in Wych Street near Drury Lane. That was the Olympic Theatre. Soon afterwards the Adelphi was opened by a speculative dye-merchant.

The actors in these popular theatres were a race unto their own. On the Victorian stage there was more scope for what is now called character work. There was no type-casting. The actor with an aquiline nose did not always have an aquiline part. The villain was always the villain; his contract said so. He had to transform himself from week to week from William Corder, tall, debonair and sinister swell, to Quilp the demoniac dwarf.

The authors of melodrama were almost as peculiar as the actors. Till the time of Buckstone, who created the genre known as 'Adelphi melodrama', they were not even respectable. They wrote quickly and according to a formula which the actors knew well. Sometimes the actors would be given a play without words; they were told roughly what they had to say and when they had to say it; but the audience was thrilled just the same.

Though the writers for the minor London theatres worked under conditions not quite so strained as those in the provinces and in portable theatres, their lives were not altogether dissimilar. Their writing was adapted in the manner which would best please the known taste of their patrons. At Sadler's Wells they liked sailors and hornpipes wherever possible; there was a large tank beneath the stage on which they floated real boats. At Hoxton they liked equestrian scenes to be introduced; horses were ridden across the stage, round the theatre and back again. Shoreditch preferred simple seduction unmixed with graver excitements. At the City of London Theatre the manager was fortunate enough to be able to hire a couple of performing elephants, and plays were adapted to suit their particular tricks. Altogether it was a joyous democracy; all were in effect equal – elephant trainer, author, actor and the conductor of the band. The play was in a real sense a result of team work.

from the Introduction to the 1928 edition
by Montagu Slater

PRODUCTION NOTES

In the Cast of *Maria Marten*, only the Juvenile Lead (gent) and the Aristocratic Old Woman are missing from the typical Victorian company. Sometimes the juvenile lead would play Pharos Lee, a part given here to the Walking Gent, who is best described in his typical part as 'Charles's Friend', a young man with an air, in short, and not much to say for himself.

The play was dressed in any period the wardrobe could best supply. There was a preference for giving Corder a really good topper and kid gloves, to make him the more recognizable. Tim Bobbin lacks description, because just as we might say 'a Buster Keaton part', a Victorian manager would say 'a Tim Bobbin part'. Tim became the type of all comic countrymen.

Some of the people have Wagnerian motifs. Tim's is 'Dosta say so?' Corder's is 'Curse the Girl!' They are often written in the script in inverted commas, and they are intended to be repeated with a variety of intonation and expression at any suitable pause in the action.

For the most part the music was left to the discretion of the musical director of the theatre. He had his own favourite pieces for his 'Hurries', his 'Combat Music', his 'Storm Music', his 'Soft Music', and trotted them out according to situation, whatever might be the play. Unfortunately there is no music of the Maria period extant.

Maria Marten

or

the murder in the red barn

LIST OF CHARACTERS

WILLIAM CORDER, Squire of Polestead's son, *Heavy Lead*
MISTER MARTEN, an honest rustic, *Heavy Father*
ISHMAEL LEE, an old gipsy-man, *2nd Heavy Man*
PHAROS LEE, his son, *Walking Gent*
TIM BOBBIN, *1st Low Comedian*
MARK ⎱
AMOS ⎰ gipsies, *Utility Gents*
FLATCATCHER ⎫   *2nd Low Comedian*
TOBERSLOPER ⎬ showmen at the fair   *3rd Low Comedian*
JACKO ⎭   *Utility Gent*
MARIA MARTEN, daughter to Mister Marten, *Leading Lady*
DAME MARTEN, her mother, *Character Old Woman*
ANNE, her sister, *Chambermaid*
   VILLAGERS, GIPSIES, &c., *Utility Ladies and Gents*

ACT ONE

SCENE ONE

Exterior of Mister Marten's Cottage.
A festive occasion. Villagers discovered dancing a Sir Roger De Coverly on the Green. MARIA MARTEN *leading the dance; close behind her* TIM BOBBIN, *and* ANNE *her Sister. Older people standing round. Music from a single fiddle and a cornet. At end of dance* TIM *breaks away and slaps his thigh.*

TIM: Dang me I never felt as happy since the day I was breeched.

ANNE: Shut thee mouth, fule!

    First bars of the Villain's music heard in the distance. WILLIAM CORDER *enters at back. He looks round and leers at* MARIA. *Villain's music grows louder.*

CORDER (*tapping leggings with riding whip in a sinister way*): Egad, that's the pretty girl who has occupied my thoughts so much since I've been here.

MARTEN: Why it's Mister Corder! I am glad to see you here, Sir, to honour our homely festivities. I heard you had arrived in our village some days ago. Will you join our merry-making?

CORDER: Thanks for your kind welcome. Who is that charming girl?

MARTEN: Why, have you forgotten her. It's my daughter Maria. (*Beckons her;* MARIA *skips towards him. Soft music.*) This is William Corder, son of our landlord.

CORDER: Miss Marten may I claim your hand for the next dance?

MARIA (*curtly*): Excuse me, Sir, but I never dance with strangers. (*Trips away, nose in the air.*)

MARTEN: You'll excuse her, Sir, she is only a country lass and doesn't know the manners of your fine London ladies, but she is an industrious girl and good as she is pretty.

TIM (*edging up sideways*): I say Mister Marten, is there anything allowed to eat? My stom jacks grumbling like an old hurdy-gurdy.

MARTEN (*throwing out his arms in a general welcome*): Come in, my friends, and enjoy yourselves with jolly old English cheer, roast beef and pudding and plenty of beer, Ha Ha!

TIM: Ecod, I'll punish the pudding and beer.

ANNE: Aye, thee great fule, thee'd punish anything.

TIM: Aye, I'll punish thee if I see thee look at that London chap.

ANNE: Me look at him? Oh what a whopper!

TIM: Yes, and I'll whop him if he winks at ye again. If thee wants to see a fine man, look at *me*.

ANNE: A fine specimen of a donkey!

TIM: Does call me a donkey?

ANNE: A regular Jack Ass.

Still quarrelling they go into the cottage followed by the rest of the party. MISTER MARTEN *left alone with* WILLIAM CORDER. *Villain's music starts again very soft.*

MARTEN: Mister Corder, can I prevail on you to join us? The fare may be humble but the welcome's great.

CORDER: I thank you, but I must return to the Farm. My Father's illness will not permit me to remain and accept your kind invitation.

MARTEN: Then good night, Mister Corder, now let us join the Merrymaking.

CORDER *alone. Villain's music; stage slowly darkens.*

CORDER: Pretty and coy, yet she shall be mine for I feel I love and have set my heart on possessing her. She seems to shrink from my advances. I must overcome her scruples. How?

Tomorrow is Polestead Fair, all the lads and lasses will assemble in the village, there must I gain an introduction to her. (*Music very loud; shouting above it.*)

> And all the arts that flattery can devise
> I'll use to make her mine (*crashing chord*).

Slinks away. ANNE *and villagers rush out of cottage, laughing.*

ANNE: Come along neighbours, lets let us have a bit of fun with Tim Bobbin, he's been telling such story lies about ghosts and goblins and murders, and he says he ain't a bit frightened and I know him to be the biggest coward in the world.

TIM (*from cottage*): Good night, Mester Marten.

ANNE: To your places lads and lasses! Giles Whackstraw, have you done as I have told you?

VILLAGER: Ees, I've made a ghost that will frighten the very devil himself.

ANNE: Hide! All of you, and we'll frighten him out of his seventeen senses.

The men hide on left, the women on the right. TIM *comes out of the cottage.*

TIM: Good night, Mester Marten, I ain't afraid you know. Good night, it be awful lonesome my walk across Churchyard! I wish as how Anne had come wi'me and I could ha' seen her back again, not as I am afraid. Oh no, I've told 'em all so, and I have been telling 'em such awful stories about ghostesses and goblinesses. I've frightened 'em all into fits, and ecod I've frightened myself too. I wish I was across the Churchyard. I've had plenty of beer to keep up my courage but it seems to have gone into my boots. I'd better be going. I'll go this way.

He goes towards the right. There is an eerie groan.

TIM: Oh, Sir, that's one of them ghostesses, I ain't frightened. Go away Measter Ghost. (*Girls groan.*) I'd better go t'other way. (*Men groan. Very loud chromatic scales.*) Oh Murder! there's more ghostesses! Go away, I'm not at home, call again tomorrow (*groan*). Oh Murder, Murder, wait till I've said my prayers, them's big ghosts here, I'll try and get by these little ones.

As he goes to the right, NAN *and the girls meet him with their aprons over their faces.* TIM, *frightened, runs to the left.*

TIM: Oh lor, Oh lor.

Enter Villager with a sheet and mask on a pole. TIM *falls down frightened. Villagers uncover and laugh.*

ANNE: Ah, you great coward, whose frightened now!

TIM (*rising*): Not me! I knew all about it. Ha, Ha, Ha!

They all laugh and the scene closes in.

CURTAIN

SCENE TWO

A wood. Wild Gipsy music heard in the distance. ISHMAEL *the Gipsy marches into the centre of the stage.*

ISHMAEL: Once more in the village where I spent my happiest and darkest hours. It was here years gone bye we pitched our tents; joy and content dwelt with us and our Zella was the sun-shine of our hearts. It was here the betrayer saw and won her from us (*music grows wilder*) and cast her off to die, heart-broken and neglected; she returned to us, but oh, how changed our beautiful flower, she died within these arms, her last words breathing the secret of her seducer's name.

Pharos my Son swore revenge on the villain who had ruined his sister and registered an oath never to rest till his knife was buried in Corder's heart. The rash attempt brought the officers of the Law upon us, he was forced to fly to a far off land, and our tribe was scattered and dispersed. The hand of time has passed across my brow, he will not recognize me now, and the revenge which has rested for years will now burst upon the head of him who ruined and murdered my poor girl, and drove my son to exile. He comes, let me stand aside and think how my first stroke of hatred shall fall. (*Retires right.*)

WILLIAM CORDER *enters.*

CORDER: I have heard from a village girl that Maria Marten and her sister will shortly pass this way to Polestead Fair. Here, under some pretence I will accost them. I notice a number of Gipsies had pitched their tent on the Common, they bring no pleasant memories to me, for once one of their dark-eyed beauties was partner of my journey to London. Psha, she is dead, her brother attempted my life and to escape justice fled across the sea. What have I to fear? There is not one of them know me now. Who have we here? (*Peering at* ISHMAEL *out of the tail of his eye.*) A Gipsy by his dress. Ah, a plan flashes across my mind; I'll employ him to get into conversation with Maria, tell her fortune. By these means she may be more easily won to my wishes. Hark ye, Gipsy, do you want to earn a gold piece?

Fiddles tremolo.

ISHMAEL: Yes, good gentleman, what is it you require, shall the poor old gipsy read the Stars for you and tell you of the future?

CORDER: No, I don't believe in your Gipsy nonsense but I wish you to accost a young girl I love.

ISHMAEL (*aside*): Ah, another victim! (*Aloud.*) What would the noble gentleman require me to say to the young lady?

CORDER: To speak to her of the future. Tell her fortune – tell her there is a gentleman who loves her and say the one who met her at the village dance, tell her not to be so shy of him, that he means honourable and that riches and happiness are before her.

ISHMAEL: I will do this never fear.

CORDER: Do your work well and you will find me a liberal master. By jove they are coming down the Lane, don't mistake, the taller of the two.

Exit CORDER.

ISHMAEL: So the wolf is abroad. Shall another innocent girl fall a victim to his desires? What matter, she is not of our people, and what mercy did the white race ever show to us? Have they not driven us from village to village, chained and imprisoned us? I'll aid this William, in doing so, further my revenge. I'll lead him on, step by step, till he mounts the scaffold. (*Tremolo, crashing chord.* ISHMAEL *shouts.*) Aye, that will be a glorious revenge.

He retires right.

Enter TIM, MARIA *and* ANNE *from the left.*

ANNE: Come along, Tim. How slow you walk.

TIM: It's the weight of money I've got in my pocket that keeps me back.

MARIA: Then I hope you'll buy us something nice at the Fair.

TIM: Yes. I'll treat you both in the swing boats, them as goes up one side and comes down t'other, and I'll buy you a pen'oth o' nuts to crack to sharpen your teeth with, and ye shall see all the shows, the moving wax work, the wild beasts, the seven legged calf and the fat woman.

MARIA: Will you treat us to all that?

TIM: I should think so, I've got a power o' brass. (*Aside.*) I've got naught but a shilling.

MARIA: Come along, Tim, we shall be talking here till the show is over.

ISHMAEL (*advancing*): Stay good people, have your fortune told?

TIM: How much is it old man?

ISHMAEL: Cross my hand with silver and I will tell you the future in store for you, cross my hand.

TIM: Oh, my bob, Oh, my bob, it's going. If I could only get away.

ANNE: Do treat us, Tim, it won't cost much for me and Maria.

TIM: Ask the old chap all about it. (*As* ANNE *turns to the Gipsy* TIM *whispers.*) Now is my time, I'll go and get my bob changed into four threepenny bits.

    Creeps off unseen.

ANNE (*who has been whispering with the Gipsy*): And can you tell us all that? Oh, Tim – why, he's gone, there he goes into that public house, I'll have him out o' that, making a fool of me, and currycomb his hair for him!

    She goes after TIM.

MARIA: How foolish of my sister to run away and leave me with this man! I'll follow her and—

ISHMAEL (*stays her*): Stay girl!

MARIA: Why stay at your bidding, what mean you?

ISHMAEL: No harm, but perhaps your future good.

MARIA: I have no belief in your stories and if I had I am too poor to tempt your skill.

ISHMAEL: I seek no reward but will tell you . . .

    Tempestuous music which grows quicker and louder to end of speech. ISHMAEL *passes his hand across his brow then seizes* MARIA's *hand.*

ISHMAEL: The Star of your destiny shines out bright and clear, today you met one who will be your fate, he loves you, is rich and prosperous and *may* make you happy – but –

> Listen and learn ere it be too late.
> Tis written upon the tables of fate
> Fortune and wealth for thee are in store,
> But your Star is shadowed, I'll read no more
> Happiness too, are here to show,
> But in the end there's – death and woe.
> Listen and be warned ere it be too late,
> At the old Red Barn shall you meet your fate.

Chord off. ISHMAEL *vanishes.*

MARIA: What, gone? He has quite taken my breath away. What did he say, I'm loved by a fine gentleman? By his description he means Mr William Corder our Landlord's Son. Oh, how nice it would be to be a rich lady, but then in the end he spoke of *Death and Woe*. Death comes to all but Woe is only caused by those who bring wretchedness upon themselves. (*Soft music.*) I have been taught those lessons of Virtue and Piety in a Village Church, that I think I can stand between Vice, and keep my name and honour spotless.

    Re-enter TIM *and* ANNE. *Trombones.*

TIM: What's quarrelling about?

ANNE: Why you're a nasty shabby fellow to run away and leave me and Maria with an old Gipsy.

TIM: He, he! I went to get all my gold changed to silver.

ANNE: Thee'st got naught by brass in thee face. Oh, Maria did you have your fortune told?

MARIA: Nonsense, I don't believe in such rubbish.

TIM: Nay, nor I, that's why I wouldn't waste my bob, I mean my sovereign.

ANNE: I don't believe you've got any money.

TIM: Yes, I've got a bob.

ANNE: Only a bob, and thou told'st me thou'st got heaps of gold.

TIM: Do you think I bring all my money out wi' me at once to lose it?

MARIA: What are you going to buy us for a fairing?

TIM: Why, Maria, I will buy thee a monkey up a stick.

ANNE: She don't want one, Tim, while you are with her.

TIM: Ah! ye dinna say so.

ANNE: And what will you buy me?

TIM: I'll buy thee a cradle.

ANNE: A cradle, what for?

TIM: Again we get married – to buy you summit as pretty as my son to put in it.

ANNE: Pretty, why you be as ugly as sin.

TIM: Then what are you sticking up to me for?

ANNE: 'Cos I know thou art that ugly I can keep thee to my sen, for thy face would frighten away any other lass.

TIM: My Mother said I was prettiest duck in flock.

ANNE: That's why thee'st grown up such an ugly goose.

MARIA: Don't quarrel, but if we are going to the Fair let's start at once or go home.

TIM: Nay, we mun go to Fair 'cos there's a public house on road and I'll treat you.

BOTH: To what?

TIM: A quart of beer.

BOTH: We don't drink beer.

TIM: Well then, you'll have a pleasure.

ANNE: What pleasure?

TIM: Why, pleasure o' seeing me drink it.

CURTAIN

SCENE THREE

Polestead village green. A Booth on each side of the stage. FLAT-CATCHER *and* TOBER-SLOPER, *two showmen, discovered.*

FLATCATCHER: Now then, Cully, open your eyes and unbutten your Hoptics.

TOBER: You shut your trap and dash your worries. What's the row?

FLAT: None, only what you are making. What's your game this time?

TOBER: I'm going in for the Fat Woman.

FLAT: And I'm going in for the living skeleton.

TOBER: Why, yer ain't got one.

FLAT: Well, I can make one. Where's yer Fat Woman?

TOBER: I'm going to stuff one.

FLAT: Then nanty wheezing, or I'll queer yer pitch.

TOBER: Do, and I'll tell the quaester you sloped your tober.

FLAT: Do you want your head swelling?

TOBER: You want your eyes dotting.

FLAT: Beware, I'll make you sing out to the public you're the double headed Nightingale.

TOBER: And you'll yell out you're a travelling Undertaker's shop and have samples of the mourning in yer eyes.

They begin to fight.

Enter JACKO, *an assistant Showman.*

JACKO: Hallo, what's the rumpus, what's the shindy?

TOBER: Come out o' that and be made into something!

JACKO: I think I've been made into everything, I've been the sea serpent, Ciscodell of the Nile, the spotted man and—

TOBER: Now you've got to be the Fat Woman.

JACKO: Fat? I ain't had no breakfast and you won't get enough fat out of me to grease the waggon wheels.

FLATCATCHER *paints a skeleton on a board.*

TOBER: Ha, ha, Flatcatcher, what are you drawing?

FLAT: Your likeness, Mr Tober-Sloper.

TOBER: Why, you've left a rib out of your skeleton.

FLAT: Yes, I've left it out for you to make your fat women with.

JACKO: What are you going to do with me?

TOBER: Stuff you.

JACKO: I wish you'd stuff me with a jolly good beef steak.

TOBER: Come, come, let's make you into a woman.

JACKO: Do I look like a woman?

They transform JACKO *elaborately.*

FLAT: Hallo, here's the crowd coming now. It's going to be pitch for pitch or H-oposition.

TOBER: H-oposition, war to the carving knife.

FLAT: Look out then or I'll warm your onion.

They begin to fight.

JACKO (*ringing a bell*): Hi, hi, a penny extra to see the rival Managers of Drury Lane and Covent Garden in a deadly duel.

TOBER: You'll get inside (*pushing him into the booth*). I'll settle with you when the slang's over tonight.

FLAT: Oh, I can lick you and your fat woman into the bargain.

They get on steps in front of booths. FLAT *beats drum and* TOBER *rings bell.*

Enter ANNE, TIM, DAME MARTEN *and a crowd of Villagers.*

TIM: He, he, he, what be that?

TOBER: The greatest sight of the present age, Madam Dona-omeequislycarsa, *the* Great Russian Giantess, can't speak a word of English, so fat and weighty that a ship had to be built expressly to bring her to this country. She measures 13 yards round the waist one yard round the ankle, weighs 18 ton and stands 16 feet 6 inches in her stocking feet.

FLAT: Don't believe him, don't believe him, I have the greatest novelty of the age, a living skeleton alive and well, eats like a horse, drinks like a fish and never gets any fatter, and he consumes 199 lbs of fresh meat daily – drinks 14 pails of water and you can hear his bones rattle as he walks round the show. This strange freak of nature is a native of Longtown-Funny in Siberia, and he ran all the way from that country to England and came at such a rate that he ran all the flesh off his bones. The charge is only a penny, don't miss a treat.

TOBER: Mine's a ligitimate performance.

FLAT: Mine's a Variety Entertainment.

TOBER: Beware of that Flycatcher!

FLAT: Beware of that catch penny!

TOBER: All in to begin, those who wish to see an instructive entertainment, don't miss this! There's a few Ladies and Gentlemen inside. The charge is only a penny all in to begin.

FLAT: Hi, hi, hi, Novelty, Novelty, Novelty.

TIM: Eh, Nan, I would like to see that fat woman.

ANNE: So should I, Tim.

TIM: Hast got any money?

ANNE: Nay, you said you'd treat us.

TIM: So I did to a quart of beer, and a pen'oth of nuts.

ANNE: You drank the one and ate t'other, hast got no money?

TIM: I lost all my money out of a hole in my pocket. I've only got three half pennies.

ANNE: I say Maester how much is it?

TOBER: One penny each, just going to begin.

ANNE: Can you let two little'uns in for three ha'pence?

TOBER: No, *One* penny is the lowest price.

TIM: Nan you keep him here while I get in.

ANNE (*winks at Showman and beckons him from door*): Shall we see all you tell us?

> TIM *creeps in.*

TOBER: Yes, my dear, so make haste or you'll be too late.

ANNE: There's my penny. Ha, Ha, two in for a penny, that's saved a ha'penny.

> *Exit into the booth.*

TOBER: What do you think now Mr Flatcatcher?

FLAT: I'll have 'em when they come out of your show.

> *Exit into his own booth.*

TOBER: Hi, hi, just going to begin. (*Exit.*)

> *Enter* MARIA.

MARIA: In the crush I got separated from my sister Annie and though I have searched the Fair I cannot find her. I feel strangely out of place here alone. I think I will return home.

> *As she is going there are faint strains of the Villain's music.*

MARIA: Ah, the gentleman coming asked me to dance with him, the very one the Gipsy spoke of. How my heart beats! I feel I want to fly . . . his presence . . . yet . . . something keeps me on this spot.

WILLIAM CORDER *strides on.*

CORDER: She is there again and if the Gipsy has fulfilled his part, matters stand easy for my wooing! Miss Marten, I am glad to see you at the Fair, but I see you have no one to escort you round. Will you accept my humble services?

MARIA:, Oh Sir, what will people say to see Maria Marten the poor labourer's daughter in company with the son of the rich Mr Corder?

CORDER: Why, that William Corder has too much manhood to see a poor girl go unprotected in a scene of wild confusion. Come, shall I take you in these shows?

MARIA: No, thank you, Mister Corder, I have no wish for such sights, but if you will aid me to find my sister I shall be thankful.

CORDER: With pleasure and as we pass along I'll tell you of the difference of these Rural sports and the gay sights of London, the balls, concerts, theatres and joys that make life worth living.

MARIA: Oh, how I should love to live in London.

CORDER: Who knows, you may.

MARIA: Mister Corder, Sir —

CORDER: At least promise me that if you do not find your sister you will allow me to see you safely home.

MARIA: I thank you, the road is somewhat lonely and —

CORDER: And among these drunken labourers and gipsy vagrants you will find a protector – nay no refusal. I'll see you safely to your own door (*aside*) and SO IS MY FIRST STEP GAINED.

Chord. Thunder. Mysterious appearance of ISHMAEL.

ISHMAEL (*Gipsy's music*): Aye, your first step towards the ladder of crime you are about to mount. When you have reached the summit then my cup of vengeance will be filled, ha, ha.

Lights up. The crowds pour out of the booths shouting 'It's a swindle', etc.

TOBER (*ringing his bell*): Hear what the people say. The only show in the Fair.

FLAT (*beating his drum*): Now good people, what did I tell you, mine is the only show worth seeing, this way the living skeleton – just going to begin.

They all go into the FLATCATCHER'S *booth.* TIM *and* ANNE *left alone on the stage.*

ANNE: Tim, are we going in there?

TIM: I've spent my last brown.

ANNE: You are a fine fellow to come to a Fair – I've got tuppence.

TIM: I've swindled t'other chap, let's try this one.

They go to the door of the booth. Met by FLATCATCHER.

FLAT: No, no, mine fine fellow. I saw you try and bilk t'other show, but you don't bilk me. Where's your money?

ANNE: Here it is.

They go inside.

TIM (*inside*): I say Measter, where's this monkey's tail?

FLAT: Oh, he comes from a land where they don't grow them. (*Wags his head at* TOBER-SLOPER.) You'll see, I've got them this time.

TOBER: And much good may it do you.

FLAT: As much as it will do you.

TOBER: Be careful or I'll tell them your living skeleton is a half-starved monkey.

FLAT: And I'll expose your fat woman stuffed with sawdust.

TOBER: I can knock sawdust out of you.

FLAT: Can you? Try it on.

They begin to fight. The people pour out of the booths.

TIM: Oh, here's a lark! Now we can see all the show for nothing.

He runs off and drags on the Fat Woman. The Villagers pull pillows from under her clothes and beat the showman. The curtain falls on a riotous scene.

CURTAIN

ACT TWO

SCENE ONE

A wood near the Gipsy encampment.
Enter ISHMAEL.

ISH: So far my plans succeeded beyond my hopes.
     Maria Marten has fallen Corder's victim,
     A child the off-spring of her shame is born,
     And William already wearies of his toy.
     Last night he came to our tents to purchase
     A deadly poison known only to our tribe.
     The child I hear is ill, I have my thoughts.
     By appointment I meet him here. . . .
     Oh! I'll watch him like a lynx, for the stars tell me
     The hour of retribution is at hand.
     Enter CORDER.

CORDER: Have you procured the drug of which we spoke?

ISH: The poison, yes!

CORDER: And can you answer for its effect?

ISH: I can, I have seen it used on man and beast.

CORDER: You know for what purpose I require it?

ISH: It matters little to me, so long as you pay me well, but you told me it was to destroy a favourite dog.

CORDER: Yes, there has been great complaint by the farmers about it destroying their flocks and I want its death to be sharp and sudden so it shall not suffer no misery.

ISH: One drop of that is sufficient to kill twenty men. Its effect is swift and sudden as the lightning, leaving no trace of its deadly work, and oft has defied the most learned doctors' skill.

CORDER: 'Tis well, here is the gold I promised, now go, let our paths from this moment be divided, and forget if you can, ever seeing my face. Nay, there is more gold (*gives him a purse*) but henceforth we are strangers.

ISH: Be it so, farewell, kind generous sir, farewell! (*Aside.*) Now will I watch his every action, I'll watch, I'll watch.

Exit.

CORDER (*loud music*): This poison must I use tonight. Maria writes the child is ill. It must die for both our safety's sake. As yet the villagers know not the child's Maria's but think 'tis one she has taken in to nurse. *Should* all be known – my father with his strict ideas of honour and virtue might drive me from his home and cut me from his will. The child shall die tonight, and Maria shall be my accomplice. I bury it in the wood, for an inquest might reveal that to the world I would not have known. Maria may have scruples, if so, it shall be the child my first victim, the mother fall my second.

Exit.

ISH (*re-enters*): 'Tis as I suspected, he takes the path towards the house he has lodged Maria Marten in to hide her shame. Now is my vengeance about to triumph, look down spirit of my heartbroken Zella from thy home among the stars, and steel thy father's heart to make thy betrayer's scaffold thy monument.

Exit.

CURTAIN

SCENE TWO

Interior of a cottage. MARIA *discovered rocking a cradle.*

MARIA: Another day passes and he comes not. Oh, my child, my child, would that thy heartbroken mother and thyself could

sink to sleep and peace for ever. Twelve months this day I was a happy village girl. Today what am I? A betrayed, a ruined woman, thus scorned'of all who knew my shame. Oh, my poor old Father, what disgrace have I not brought on thee, but William shall marry me, I hold his promise, he shall give me back . . . (*Villain's music, very soft and slow. She starts and cries out.*) . . . my honour!! or . . . (*Bursts into tears. Some one is hammering on the door. She lifts her head.*) Oh, perhaps it is he —
    Enter ANNE *and* TIM. *Trombones.*

ANNE: No, it's me.

TIM: And it's me, too.

MARIA: Anne, my sister.

TIM: Yes, and Tim thy Brother-in-Law that is to be.

ANNE: Shut up – I was going by and called in to see thee.

TIM: Yes, and I called in to see thee baby.

ANNE: Get off, what's thee want with the baby!

TIM: Why to get my hand in, to be sure, yes and I be going to be married to be sure and you can't account for accidents.
    Goes to the cradle.

MARIA: Nan, I hope you have kept my secret. So far all think the child one I have taken in to nurse. You have told no one different?

ANNE: No, I have told no one but Tim.

TIM: Yes, and I've told no one but Brother Bob and sixteen of my cousins.

ANNE: Oh, thou great fule! But Maria, Mother and Father be coming soon so I thought I'd just tell you so as you might be ready for 'em.

MARIA: No, no, don't let them see me in my shame. My Mother's grey hair will seem to speak reproaches, and tell of her past virtuous life, now disgraced by my misdeed, my Father – I should die beneath his stern gaze.

ANNE: Come, come, cheer up Maria, it won't be so bad as you think, I've broke the news to our parents and though they cried at first, Mother said you were still her child, though fallen in sin through a villain's means.

TIM: Ah, ah, here be a sight. This kid's opening its mouth and got no teeth.

ANNE: Get along, little'uns like that ain't got no teeth.

TIM: Then how do they eat their bread and butter? Oh, oh, oh, its head is as bald as a duck egg. Run Nan and borrow my grandfather's wig.

ANNE: Get along, it don't want no wig.

TIM: But I tell you, it's a bald yedded yun'un. Eh, now it's opening its mouth. Gie it the knob of the kitchen poker to suck.

ANNE: Don't want to make the baby as big a fule as thee. Thy mother used to gie thee the knob o' the wooden bedstead to suck and, thee'st been wooden headed ever since. (*A knock.*) That's the old folks. Tim.

TIM: I want to stop and nurse the baby.

ANNE: Nonsense, you will drop it and gie it the gravel rash.

TIM: I never saw such a funny thing of a little baby afore, it got no teeth, it canna speak and it's bald yedded, but it's just like William Corder, I can tell it by its nose.

NAN *and* TIM *go out.*

MARIA: My Father and Mother coming! Oh, how I dread the meeting, and when I think of home a frowning form appears to guard the threshold shrieking in my ear! ! 'Hence thou shalt not enter here!' Heart be firm, they come.

Enter MARTEN *and* DAME.

MARIA *falls on her knees. Soft music.*

MARIA: Once more do I see the faces of those dear to me. Father, Mother, your unhappy child implores forgiveness.

DAME: Unhappy girl, a Mother's heart is more indulgent than the World's, but there is yet one to be appeased, your Father.

MARTEN: What your miseries are I well can guess, what a Father's sufferings are, I too well know. Oh, how I doted on thee

Daughter, words cannot speak, yet you sacrificed me for a villain. Your ingratitude has bleached my head and broken my heart.

MARIA: No more, in Mercy. Oh, no more!

MARTEN: As I gaze on thee I think of thy infant days when first your little steps began, when laughingly with extended arms you ran towards me and I trembled lest your feet should fail. (*Soft music.*) You escaped those and a thousand dangers, but now you fall, fall to earth never to rise.

> *The weeping Mother raises* MARIA *from her knees.*

DAME: But our child is repentant, she faints with shame and grief. Do speak a word of comfort to her and sooth her anguish.

MARTEN: Did I not rear her in domestic tenderness,
   Train her in paths of virtue?
   Did I not press her to this doting heart,
   And in my foolish pride proclaim my child
   A paragon of earth! . .
             And did she not blast
   All my fond hopes and clinging to a villain
   Leave me in my storm of grief. Oh! I feel that I
   Could curse —

MARIA (*kneeling again*): No, no, your vengeance cannot make you deaf
   To the agony of a despairing child!
   Behold me on my knees . . .
   I bring the sacrifice of a broken heart.

I don't ask your love till you know I am worthy of your love, and I do not ask your confidence till you feel again I can be trusted, but do not deny me the shelter of your paternal roof.

DAME: Dear Husband, do not aggravate the dear girl's misery, she is repentant, she is the shorn lamb, temper the storm to her affliction, but do not add another wound to her heart already lacerated.

MARIA: Bless you, Mother, bless you for these words.

MARTEN: Arise, Maria, I forgive thee. We are all sinners and should be merciful in our judgment to each other.
> Thy Father's arm,
> Thy Father's home,
> Are open to receive thee.

They fall into each other's arms.

DAME: Come child, return to your home at once.

MARIA: I cannot, I am awaiting the arrival of William.

MARTEN: Believe not in that villain who has thus deceived, betrayed thee.

MARIA: Nay, he has sworn to marry me a thousand times, I hold his written promise. It is only for family reasons our union has been delayed. He may be here at any moment.

DAME: Come Marten, we will leave her now, she may wish to see William on important matters. Let us hope for the best, have patience.

MARTEN: Hope? I am
> The scathed tree of the heath, that cannot drop.
> The bolt that struck my branches off, has left
> My trunk erect in wretched loneliness.

Exit DAME and MARTEN.

MARIA: My Father's forgiveness has lightened my heart. Oh, that William would fulfil his promise, happiness would then be mine. Ah, 'tis he!

Enter WILLIAM. Tremolo Fiddles.

CORDER: Dear Maria, I received your note and hasten to you. How is the child?

MARIA: Ill, very ill, I fear it is not long for this world, and if you do not make me an honourable woman would that I could share its fate!

CORDER: Have I not sworn by every sacred tie you shall be my wife. My Father hovers o'er the grave – he dead, I'll make you mine at once and our child shall be a bond of happiness to our union.

MARIA: Dear William, I do believe you.

CORDER: Nay, I swear it!

They embrace. Mysterious appearance of ISHMAEL *at the window.*

MARIA: Why have you not brought the doctor as I requested?

CORDER: Today he could not attend, he will call tomorrow. I showed him your note and he mixed this small bottle and said for the present it would remove all pain.

MARIA: Thanks, dear William. I will administer it at once.

CORDER: Do so, Maria.

She gives the medicine to the child. The music rises to a storm.

MARIA: The little one seems soothed already. Oh, William, my Father and Mother have been here almost broken hearted at my shame.

CORDER: Fear not, dear girl, all will yet be well. But see, the child!

MARIA: Oh what ails it! 'Tis convulsed! (*Screams.*) 'tis dead. (*Falls across cradle.*)

CORDER: Dead, then I am safe.

ISHMAEL (*at window*): No, lost eternally in the sight of heaven. Another step on the ladder of crime.

Gipsy music.

CURTAIN

SCENE THREE

A wood. Enter FLATCATCHER.

FLAT: I am an bankrupt, I lost my show, my living skeleton walked off with my monkey and brought my pigs to a pretty market so I have taken to the road like bold Dick Turpin and the first man I see I shall rob. Ah, a rustic comes. Back, back, until a proper time. (*He hides.*)

    Enter TIM.

TIM: Dang me if I like coming out at night when it's dark, only old Marten would make me go and pay his rent, as Squire had sent for it and he's three weeks behind, so I better get my legs on the road.

FLAT (*springs out and presents pistol*): Now, stand and deliver.

TIM: You made me all of a shiver.

FLAT: Your money or your life.

TIM: Nay, take my life and spare my money.

FLAT: Ha, you have money, I can see it in your face.

TIM: Then take it out of my face.

FLAT: Come, turn out all you've got.

TIM: Oh, Measter Marten, Measter Marten, your rent's going. (*It goes.*)

FLAT: Good, now let's have your jewellery.

TIM: There's my pipe and my bacca box and an old horse nail as I open the stable door with.

FLAT: Now, you can go.

TIM: I say Measter Highwayman you might do something for us.

FLAT: What is it?

TIM: Just shoot through my hat and coat for I be reckoned very brave in our village and I shouldn't like old Marten to think that I had given up his money without a tussle.

FLAT: Very well, I'll oblige you. Hold up your hat.

    He shoots it.

TIM: Now through my smock (FLAT *fires*). Beautiful, now through the other side.

FLAT: I've got no more powder, I can't.

TIM: Oh, try, oh, try.

FLAT: What's the use, it would only miss fire?

TIM: Would it, then here's a pistol what never misses fire. (*Draws out a cudgel.*) Now give me my money back – now my jewellery, my pipe, my bacca bòx and horse nail, and now gie me all you've got about you.

FLAT: Let me go.

TIM: Yes, I will, you shall go to the lock up and I'll watch you every inch of the way.

Exit beating FLATCATCHER.

SCENE FOUR

A secret part of the wood.
WILLIAM *and* MARIA *discovered burying the child.*

MARIA: William, William, this is a fearful deed.

CORDER: But it must be done for both our safeties.

MARIA: My poor infant, to be buried like a dog, no prayers above its little head, far from the shadow of the Church, to leave it here within this Wood it's terrible.

CORDER: 'Tis for the best, believe me. An inquest might tell more than we should like the world to know.

MARIA: Ah? Then the child has not come to its sudden death by fair means?

CORDER: How should I know, if a mistake has been made, it lies with the doctor not myself.

MARIA: Oh! What horrible suspicions cross my mind!

CORDER: Then let suspicion die, for a magistrate's enquiry would harm you more than myself. Remember the penalty of concealment of birth.

MARIA: I am in your power and have no will of my own, but it's hard for my little one to be here.

CORDER: Nonsense, the child will sleep peaceful as in a Church-yard. See, I have marked this tree so that at eventide you can strew the little grave with flowers.

MARIA: Oh, take me, take me quickly from this fearful spot.

CORDER: Come then, how you tremble! Nonsense, girl! No eye beholds us.

ISHMAEL (*in the distance*): Yes, the eye of Ishmael the Gipsy.

CURTAIN

SCENE FIVE

Another part of the wood. Enter MARK *and* AMOS, *leading a band of Gipsies.*

MARK: Yes, my brother, we have been driven from the Common by the Officers of the Law, acting for this William Corder, but before we go we'll have vengeance full and deep.

GIPSIES: Vengeance, Vengeance!

MARK: Fear not, but strike the blow surely, and with a firm hand. They heeded not the cries of our wives and children, why then should we spare his life? This night Corder's eyes shall be closed in the sleep of death.

GIPSIES: Ah, Vengeance, Vengeance.

They are about to rush off when ISHMAEL *enters.*

ISHMAEL: Hold children, whither go ye?

MARK: For vengeance. This William Corder has set the police upon us, hunted us like wild beasts from the land his good father allowed us to pitch our tents on, and for resistance to the

Law many of our tribe lie in the Jail, so Corder's life shall answer for it.

ISHMAEL: Hold, hold, I say this must not be.

MARK AND GIPSIES: What do you mean?

ISHMAEL: That vengeance on Corder belongs to me.

WILLIAM CORDER *appears in the distance.*

CORDER: Ah, my name, those rascally Gipsies, I'll listen. (*Hides.*)

ISHMAEL: All the wrongs you cry of are but pigmies to the great wrong that Corder did to me. He robbed me of my dearest child Zella and sent her brother a wanderer across the sea. For these deeds I'll make him an outcast, strip him of fortune, and let him suffer the pangs of despised beggary we suffer, drag him to the scaffold foot, then with my vengeful eyes glaring in his and my cry of bitter mockery ringing in his ears, I'll force him to mount step by step till I place the rope about his neck. This will be my revenge, a long and torturing one. Your's would be too quick, too painless.

MARK: Our brothers cry for vengeance within their prison cells. Shall they cry in vain?

ISHMAEL: Not so. He has stacks of wheat and hay – give them – nay barns, house, all, to the flames, make him a beggar, and that complete. I will reveal a secret that will put the rope round his neck. Nay, away, I will not tell you my secret yet, until your work of desolation will be complete, then come to the father of your tribe and I will give you proof shall drag Corder to a murderer's doom.

MARK: Aye, friends, 'tis a glorious plan. Before we strike our tents the light to guide us on our road shall be the blazing embers of Corder's home.

Gipsies go out.

ISHMAEL: Ha, ha, vengeance has come at last after years of watching and waiting, I'll follow and see how my trusty dogs mark down my game.

Exit.

CORDER (*coming from behind a tree*): The old traitor, it is lucky I overheard them. So the old man is Zella's father. Can he have watched me bury the child? If so he is the only witness for Maria dare not speak. I'll cross the fields and reach the farm before them. My gun is loaded and I'll find means to silence this one witness against me.

CURTAIN

SCENE SIX

A farm yard. Enter Gipsies with torches.

MARK: This way brothers, I hear the servants are in the village, Corder is from home. Now's our time. But should he return, we hurl him into the blazing fire. Remember, dead men tell no tales, this way, this way.

   They go behind the Farm buildings.
   Enter ISHMAEL.

ISHMAEL: Brave boys, there at their work, soon all will be a heap of ruin, ha, ha. The Farm in darkness, where can Corder be?

   Enter CORDER *with a gun.*

CORDER: Here, old traitor, Dog – villain you would betray me.
ISHMAEL: Aye, I would drive you a beggar from your home.
CORDER: Ah, ah, that threat I laugh at, the Farm and all's insured to its full value so they can go to the devil.
ISHMAEL: But your life is in my power. I am the father of that poor girl whose soul you so basely betrayed, the father of the lad you drove to exile, I swore revenge, it is at hand. I dogged you step by step, I saw you poison Maria's child and bury it in the woods, I will take the officers there and your life is forfeit.

CORDER: So is yours old traitor. (*Shoots him.*) So perish the only witness to my crime.

Exit hurriedly.

Enter Gipsies with torches.

MARK: That shot, ah, see our father bleeds! (*They raise him.*) Who has done this?

ISHMAEL: William Corder. I am dying. Swear to seek out my son, swear by the mystic relics of our tribes, tell him to relentlessly pursue the path of vengeance until mine and his sister's death are avenged.

ALL: We swear.

ISHMAEL: 'Tis well, 'tis well, my eyes grow dim. My blood is chilled and see, the spirit of my Zella calls to my home among the stars.

MARK: But this secret you know of Corder's, reveal it to us ere you die.

ISHMAEL: Corder, he is a – a . . . (*falls back*).

MARK: The spirit is struggling to break from its earthy prison but the doors are fast, while we hang over him, our brother is in his death throes but the reluctant spirit cannot pass away, the stars have gone out, and the moon has veiled her face, lift up your voices and let every face look steadily to the WEST.

During this speech there are heard the first bars of a solemn dirge. The Gipsies kneel round ISHMAEL *who leans his dying head on* MARK'S *shoulder. The stage is lighted only by the red glare of the burning Farm. The Gipsies sing:*

> Let the dirge be sung
> And the bell be rung
> And the torch burn red
> O'er the dying one's head
> Till the spirit is free
> And the flesh is dead.

Troubled spirit pass away
From your prison house of clay,
Every door is open wide,
Night is at the turn of tide.
Pass away,
Pass away.

Darkness creeps over the scene.

CURTAIN

ACT THREE

SCENE ONE

Mister Marten's kitchen.
MARIA *discovered.*

MARIA: I wonder if William will call today. I sent a note by my brother George, begging him to come. Ah, a footstep, I know 'tis he.

    Enter CORDER *with a carpet bag.*

CORDER: Dearest Maria, on receiving your letter I hastened at once to see you.

MARIA: William, when will you keep the promise so long made to me?

CORDER: I came today to tell you, that the death of my father removed the only obstacle to our Union.

MARIA: This is indeed joyful news, I'll acquaint my parents with your tidings.

CORDER: One moment Maria, you know the aversion my Mother has to your family, therefore to keep our marriage a secret from her, I want the ceremony to be performed in London.

MARIA: London, why there?

CORDER: Business of importance calls me away this very night. You must be my companion. I wish you to put on this suit of male attire and meet me tonight at the old Red Barn.

    Tremolo Fiddles.

MARIA: No, no, not there. Even in childhood I played about it and its shadows cast a chill upon me, and did not a Gipsy at Polestead Fair warn me against the Red Barn for there I should meet my fate?

CORDER: And will not that prophecy be fulfilled, for from the Barn we start on our road to love and happiness.

MARIA: But to leave in the darkness, in male attire – why this mystery?

CORDER: I have told you, you must do this, or I must quit the village for London without you.

MARIA: I consent, I'll send my parents to you and tonight meet you in the old Red Barn.

She goes out with the carpet bag.

CORDER *alone. Stormy music.*

CORDER: She consents, one point gained, 'curse the girl'. She binds me down, my mad gambling speculations have lost me a once ample fortune, a rich marriage can only save me. Maria, when you consented to meet me in the Red Barn you sealed your doom. (*Crashing chord.*)

Enter MR MARTEN *and his* DAME.

With a grim effort CORDER *recovers himself.*

MARTEN: Ah, William is this true? Maria tells me you are about to keep your promise.

CORDER: 'Tis true Mister Marten.

DAME: I'm glad to hear it, for the poor girl has too long borne disgrace in her native place.

MARTEN: Tut, tut, wife, Mister Corder is about to act an honourable part to our child, so cease upbraiding. When will the marriage take place?

CORDER: As early as possible for tonight we both depart for London.

MARTEN AND DAME: London?

CORDER: Yes, for reasons known to ourselves, 'Family reasons', our marriage must take place there.

MARTEN: Why, William cannot you be married here?
        Here she has been pointed at in shame,
        Here the stain should be taken from her name.

DAME: Yes, why can't you be married at our village Church like me and my old man and let the fiddle be set scraping, the bells ringing and all our friends have a jollification.

CORDER: I'm sorry this cannot be. I do not wish my Mother to know of my marriage till it is over.

MARTEN: Very well, William, if Maria wishes to go with you, I'll not withhold my consent. Will you step in and have some refreshments?

DAME: Yes do, William. I've got a cold boiled ham and some fresh butter, perhaps you would like to take a bit to London with you?

CORDER: Thanks for your kindness, but I must return to the Farm, and so farewell. .

DAME: Well, good day, William, and if I can't dance at your wedding may be I'll dance at the christening. (*Exit.*)

MARTEN: I'll not detain you longer for I see you are impatient to depart. Let us hear from you on your arrival in London. Be kind to my child. She has suffered much for you, I now entrust her to your care . . . and as you deal by her so may heaven . . . deal by you.

    As he speaks CORDER *starts back, his jaw drops. His eyes protrude. Exit* MARTEN.

CORDER: Heaven? What have I got to do with heaven! The deed I contemplate will close these gates forever on me.

    (*Stage dark. Villain's music very loud.*)
    Hence, hence, remorse and every thought that's good,
    The storm that lust began must end in blood.

CURTAIN

SCENE TWO

Another part of the wood.
Enter TIM *with a bundle and a stick.*

TIM: Well, here I be, once more ready to start for Lunnon. This
makes the fourth time I've had my bundle on my back, when
somehow sommit have always happened to make I turn
whome again but now I will go. I ha'gotten three half crowns,
two silver sixpences and three ha'pence in copper. Who knows
but some grand lady wi' coach and Blackamore servant may
say, Tim bea'st a pretty lad, wilt come a be my husband? He,
he, there be no telling, so here goes.

ANNE (*heard without*): Tim, Tim.

TIM: My stars here be a stoppage, now I'd better run.
      He is going when ANNE *catches him by the collar.*

ANNE: I've catched you at last, thee'st a sad purjured false lover
and you be bent on going to Lunnon.

TIM: Eas, I be, here's a rumpus.

ANNE: Hav'nt you said again and again that I were the girl of
your heart and if you had a wife, no one but I should be
Misses Tim Bobbin.

TIM: Eas, but I said *if*, mind that.

ANNE: Then what did you make me fall in love for?

TIM: Because you couldn't help it.

ANNE: If you go to Lunnon, I'll follow you if I walk every step
of the way barefoot.

TIM: Now don't be a fool, Nan.

ANNE: You shan't make one o' me, I can tell thee Tim.

TIM: I'm only going to see the curosities, I shall come
back.

ANNE: But I'm afraid of thee for when a young man gets fra'
    the country as knows summit, he never gets away again till
    he know summit more than summit.
TIM: You don't say so. (*Aside*.) Dang me if I don't go. (*Aloud*.)
    What I see I can tell ye all about, and then you'll be as wise as
    me every bit.
ANNE: Now, I'll tell you what Tim, if thee won't go, you shall
    come to Mother's and have as much cold pudding as you can
    eat.
TIM: You don't keep cold puddin do you?
ANNE: Oh, plenty.
TIM: Well now, I never do!
ANNE: Why, thee doesn't throw it away?
TIM: No, I eat it all when it be hot.
ANNE: Come Tim, there be lumps of fat in as big as my thumb.
TIM: He, he, pull Lunnon!
    He pulls one way, she the other.
ANNE: Pull pudding!
TIM: Ecog, puddin got it.
    Song and Dance.
TIM: Lunnon's curosities tempt me away,
        Fortune may smile and pay for the trip.
ANNE: Nay, Tim, let me persuade you to stay,
        There's many a slip twixt the cup and the lip.
TIM: Talents and person be sure o' promotion
        So that you see I've two strings to my bow.
ANNE: The proverb do say twixt two stools, I've a notion
        Plump on the ground you will certainly go.
TIM: Odds, Bobs, both be so ticing,
        Lunnon and puddin I can't get away.
ANNE: You look like the donkey that stood over nice in
        Choosing between two bundles of hay.
    They go off, the stage darkens, the music changes.
    Enter CORDER.

CORDER: A dismal gloom obscures the face of day.
    Either the sun has slipped behind the cloud
    Or journeys down the West of heaven
    With more than common speed,
    To avoid the sight of what I'm about to do.
    Since I set out on this accurst design
    Wherever I tread methinks the solid earth
    Trembles beneath my feet . . .
    And yet it must be done, I must go on.
  Ah, I have forgotten to bring a pick axe and spade. Fool. Should I return my victim will escape. I'll linger here and try and borrow from some passing labourer.

    Re-enter TIM *with spade and pick axe.*

TIM: I'm nearly busted, I've had such a blow out of cold puddin, now old Marten says I must go and dig a bit of his garden. Hallo, Measter Corder.

CORDER: It seems you know me.

TIM: I ought to, brother-in-law.

CORDER: What do you mean by brother-in-law?

TIM: I knows all about it.

CORDER: It's more than I do.

TIM: I knows, brother-in-law. Thee'st going to marry Maria, and I'm going to marry Nan, so we'll be in the family-line.

CORDER (*aside*): What, I a relation of this bumkin? No – I'm more determined to take Maria's shackles from me.

TIM: What's grumbling about? I know you think you're not as good looking as I.

CORDER: Can you lend me a spade and I'll pay you for it.

TIM: What's want a spade for, brother-in-law? Art going to bury summit?

CORDER: What's that you say?

TIM: Ecod, you be as fierce as a rat without a tail. I thought the dogs had been worrying some of our sheep and thou wanted to bury him.

CORDER: No, no, a friend of mine wants me to take a young tree to plant on his estate and I wanted a spade to dig it up with.

TIM: How much will you gie I for a pick and spade?

CORDER: How much do you earn a day?

TIM: Eighteen pence and they finds me in puddin.

CORDER: Then I give you two shillings for the loan of them. Can you change a five pound note?

TIM: Who are yer getting at? I never seed one in my life.

CORDER: Can you change a sovereign?

TIM: Aye, if you will wait until I go to the public house and get a drink wi'it.

CORDER: No, no, I cannot wait. Here's a shilling and three pence in coppers and I'll give you the rest when next we meet.

TIM: Then you will owe I ninepence don't forget, you'll find the pick and spade along the lane in the tool house yonder.

CORDER: I'll leave them outside the door of the Red Barn so you can get them when you want them.

TIM: All right. Don't forget you owe I ninepence, that's one and three pence more for my own stocking. Hallo, what's that? Dang my buttons if there bean't a dandy chap kissing my Nan. I'll punch his head till it's like a pickled cabbage.

He goes to the side of the stage and watches.

Enter ANNE *with* MARIA *dressed as a man.*

MARIA: Do you think any one will recognize me as I cross the field Anne?

ANNE: Not a bit of it, you make such a jolly nice little man I could fall in love with you myself.

MARIA: Tell Mother I will write as soon as I arrive in London. Farewell, dear sister, William will be waiting. One kiss before we part. (*They embrace.*)

TIM *comes up.*

TIM: Aye, do it again, do it again, her likes it.

MARIA: Who is this booby? (*Aside.*) It's Tim, isn't it?

ANNE: Yes, he won't know you and he's jealous. Let's have a bit of fun. He's such a coward.

TIM: Now then, Mister Whipper-Snapper, what, what are you doing with that young gal?

MARIA: What's that to do with you, Mister Chawbacon?

TIM: Mind I don't chaw thy bacon, and as for you, you shamed faced hussy —

ANNE: Call me a hussy, how dare you, I never saw the chap afore in all my life.

TIM: Oh? What a whopper!

MARIA: How dare you address a young lady like that! If you speak – nay look at her again – I'll thrash you within an inch of your life.

TIM (*sparring*): Come on, come on.

MARIA: Oh, I say, Anne, the fellow will kill me.

ANNE: Don't be afraid, he's too big a coward. You touch this young man and I'll tear your eyes out.

TIM: Thee go home, or I'll tell thy mother, come on now, come on.

MARIA: I shan't take my coat off to a scarecrow like you, but beware, I'm a dab hand at singlesticks, in constant practice at the Pistol Gallery – and have had the gloves with Tom Sayers, who confessed I was a better boxer than he was.

TIM: Dang it, this chap might hurt me.

ANNE: I told you he was a coward.

MARIA (*squares*): Come on, Sir, come on.

TIM: Go on and hit one thee own size.

MARIA: You're a coward, Sir, farewell, sweet one. Kiss. (*They embrace.*)

TIM: If you kiss her again I'll —

MARIA: What, Sir?

TIM: Nothing.

MARIA: Good bye, sweet girl, and if that bumpkin annoys you, I'll come from London and with my pistol shoot him thro' and thro' like a cullender, another kiss. (*They embrace.*)

TIM: Aye, do it again. (*Exit* MARIA.)

TIM (*shouting after her*): Come back and kiss her again.
  She does. Business continued ad lib.

ANNE (*at last*): He's gone. Oh, Tim, isn't he a nice little man?

TIM: Go on, false perfidious one, kissing chap before my face, and after keeping I afraid going to Lunnon and seducing me with your cold puddin.

ANNE: Now, Tim dear.

TIM: I ain't cost thee naught, go away (*He begins to cry.*)

ANNE: Don't cry Tim.

TIM: I ain't crying, I'se pulling faces, 'cos I didn't smash that chap.

ANNE: Suppose I told you all about it.

TIM: I don't want to know any more. I've seen enough.

ANNE: Well, that wasn't a man at all.

TIM: Ah? who were it then?

ANNE: Why, my sister Maria.

TIM: Were it, he he, he, I know'd it were her all the time.

ANNE: Oh, you great big story!

TIM: Do you think if I'd hadn't known it, I wouldn't smashed her?

ANNE: Now, when are we going to get married?

TIM: I'll put the bungs up at once and go to the Blacksmith's and buy a ring.

ANNE: It must be gimlet gold like Mother's, you know.

TIM: Wi' a great big carbuncle as big as my fist, but only fancy, Maria in them things em bobs. Ecod, it beats cock-fighting.

CURTAIN

SCENE THREE

Inside the Red Barn.
CORDER *discovered digging a grave. Villain's music.*

CORDER: All is complete, I await, I await now my victim. Will
she come? Oh yes, a woman is fool enough to do anything for
the man she loves. Hark, 'tis her footstep bounding across the
fields! She comes, with hope in her heart, a song on her lips,
little does she think that death is so near.
He steps into a dark corner.
Enter MARIA. *The music turns soft and gentle.*
MARIA: William not here, where can he be, what ails me? A
weight is at my heart as if it told some evil, and this old Barn
how like a vault it looks, fear steals upon me, I tremble in every
limb. I will return to my home at once.
CORDER (*advancing*): Stay, Maria!
MARIA: I'm glad you are here. You don't know how frightened
I've been.
CORDER: Did any one see you cross the fields?
MARIA: Not a soul. I remembered your instructions.
CORDER: That's good. Now Maria do you remember a few days
ago threatening to betray me about the child to Constable
Ayers? (*Tremolo fiddles.*)
MARIA: A girlish threat made in a heat of temper, because you
refused to do justice to one you had wronged so greatly. Do
not speak of that now, let us leave this place.
CORDER: Not yet, Maria, you don't think my life is to be held at
the bidding of a silly girl. *No*, look what I have made here!
He drags her to the grave. Slow music.
MARIA: A grave. Oh, William, what do you mean?

CORDER: To kill you, bury your body there. You are a clog upon my actions, a chain that keeps me from reaching ambitious height. You are to die.

MARIA (*kneels*): But not by your hand, the hand that I have clasped in love and confidence. Oh! Think William, how much I have sacrificed for you, think of our little child above, now in heaven pleads for its mother's life. Oh spare, oh spare me!

CORDER: 'Tis useless, my mind's resolved, you die tonight.
Thunder and lightning.

MARIA: Wretch!
Since neither prayers nor tears will touch your stony heart,
Heaven will surely nerve my arm to battle for my life.
She seizes CORDER.

CORDER: Foolish girl, desist!

MARIA: Never with life!
They struggle, he shoots her, she falls in his arms.

MARIA (*soft music*):
William I am dying, your cruel hand has stilled
The heart that beat in love alone for thee.
Think not to escape the hand of justice, for
When least expected it will mark you down,
At that moment think of Maria's wrongs.
Death claims me, and with my last breath I die blessing and forgiving thee.
Dies.

CORDER: Blessing and forgiveness and for me, her (*loud music*) murderer! What have I done! Oh, Maria, awake, awake, do not look so tenderly upon me, let indignation lighten from your eyes and blast me!
Oh may this crime for ever stand accurst,
The last of murders, as it is the worst.

CURTAIN

ACT FOUR

SCENE ONE

Mister Marten's kitchen.
DAME MARTEN *sitting by the fire.*

DAME: Heigho, how strange it is day after day passes and no tidings of Maria. It is now twelve months since she left home and only two letters have we received, the first from William saying she was so much taken up with London pleasures she had no time to write, the second such strange writings so unlike hers saying she had a gathered hand and could scarce hold the pen. Ah me, I don't feel at all satisfied. Dear, dear, how sleepy I am, I'll just take forty winks in my chair here.

As she sleeps she hears soft music. Slowly the wall of the cottage fades away showing the Red Barn. She sees MARIA *enter; she sees* WILLIAM *waiting for her in the dark corner; how they quarrel, how* CORDER *raises his pistol and drags* MARIA *towards the open grave. His hand is on the trigger and as he is about to fire she wakes with a scream. The vision vanishes. The kitchen is in darkness.*

DAME (*sobbing*): Oh, this is the third time I've dreamt that terrible dream within a week. Oh Marten, Marten!

MARTEN, TIM *and* ANNE *rush in with lights.*

MARTEN: What's the matter, Dame?

ANNE: Have you dropped summit on your toes, Mother?

TIM: Nay, it's screwmatics pinched her.

DAME: Oh, Marten, I've had such a terrible dream.

MARTEN: Just what I thought, been dreaming again!

DAME: Something terrible has happened to our Maria, for this is the third time I've dreamt I saw her murdered by William Corder in the old Red Barn.

MARTEN: Nonsense, dreams are not to be believed in.

TIM: Of course not, I always dream when I be on the middle of my back.

ANNE: And I always dream of thee, Tim, when I be on my left side.

DAME: I will be satisfied as to the fate of our child. Go, Marten, summon the neighbours, get lights and search the Barn at once. What, you hesitate? Nay then, I go myself.

MARTEN: Nay, wife, stay and compose yourself. Tim will go with me.

TIM: You catch me, I'm not going ghost-hunting. Oh dear, no!

MARTEN: Come on, there's nothing to hurt you.

TIM: I don't know about that. If a young Hob Gobblin should bite my nose off, that would be a loss to my beauty.

ANNE: Go along you great, cowardy custard, and look after our poor Maria, or I won't marry thee.

TIM: And shall she marry me, Measter Marten, if I go?

MARTEN: If she likes you I'll give my consent, for you're an honest lad.

TIM: Then I'll go and get my pitchfork and stable lantern.

MARTEN: Go, Dame, lie thee down and let Annie get you something warm.

ANNE: Yes, I'll go and get thee a cup of green tay, that will settle thee nerves for thee.

DAME: Oh, husband, hasten, hasten, for I feel I cannot rest until this mystery is cleared up. (*Exit* DAME.)

MARTEN: Make haste, Tim, and follow me. (*Exit* MARTEN.)

TIM: Good bye, Nan, I be going.

ANNE: Well, go on then.

TIM: I say, Nan, you might . . .

ANNE: Might what, you fule?

TIM: Gie I a cherry numble.

ANNE: What's that?

TIM: A knockchops.

ANNE: Go on, or I'll knock they chops.

TIM: I mean a cuss.

ANNE: Oh, you wicked chap for cussing me.

TIM: I mean a kiss.

ANNE: Can't you take it, Timmy dear?

TIM: He, he, he!

MARTEN (*calling from outside*): Tim, Tim!

TIM: I'm coming, Measter Marten.

He is kissing ANNE *when* MISTER MARTEN *comes in and takes him off by the ear.*

TIM: Hold on, leave a lad alone, good bye Nan. I'm going to the murder and haven't had my kiss. (*Exit.*)

ANNE: Oh, what a fule he is. I'll have such a lark when mother goes to sleep, I'll get a sheet off my bed and run across the field and when I get to the Barn I'll frighten our Tim into fits.

CURTAIN

SCENE TWO

The Red Barn.
Enter MISTER MARTEN *and* TIM *with lanterns.*

TIM: Doan't run away, Measter Marten, I bean't frightened.

MARTEN: The old Barn has not been used for some time.

TIM: No, two or three days after Maria went away with William I came for my pick and spade, but they had been putting loads of straw in the third bay and buried 'em.

MARTEN: But the straw has been removed again.

TIM: Yes, Corder's mon took it away a month ago, but said he know'd naught about my tools. Oh, look there, Measter Marten, it's a ghost.

MARTEN: A what, Tim?

TIM: Nay, it's only a rat.

MARTEN: Hold the light here, Tim.

TIM: All right, Measter Marten.

MARTEN: What's this, a pick and spade!

TIM: Why them's mine, I can swear to 'em!

MARTEN: Ah, what's this, woman's hair on the spade, and stains like blood!

TIM: Then it bean't my spade, Measter Marten. I wish I'd got my ninepence.

MARTEN: Hold the light, Tim, something seems to tell me my wife's dream is too true.

TIM: Oh, look, here, Measter, here's a young pup of a gun.

MARTEN: A pistol, a name – William Corder – search, Tim, I feel we are about to discover a terrible crime, ah, the ground has been moved here, dig, Tim.

TIM (*trembling*): I will, but don't leave me, Measter Marten. (*Digs.*)

MARTEN: What this? A neck tie, 'tis Maria's! many a time, I've seen her wear it. Dig, Tim!

TIM: I will, don't leave me, Measter Marten. Oh! look here! Murder!

MARTEN: Ah, too true it is, basely murdered by that William Corder. Oh my poor poor child! But justice now shall take the place of tears, justice, justice!

> For if justice in England be not dead,
> This deed shall cost William Corder's head.

He rushes off.

TIM: Don't leave me, Measter Marten, I'll take care on yer.

And if justice in England be of use,
This deed shall cook Corder's Goose.

I say, Measter Marten, what gone and left me all alone with the ghostesses? Measter Marten!

Enter NAN *with sheet over her head.* TIM *yells and falls down through a trap door. Crashing chord.*

CURTAIN

ACT FIVE

SCENE ONE

Drawing Room of WILLIAM CORDER'S *London house.*
WILLIAM *alone.*

CORDER: Twelve months has past and still no one suspects me as a murderer or that the body of Maria Marten lies in the third bay of the old Barn. I have married a wealthy and accomplished lady and as soon as all is complete we will leave England for ever. I'll call the servants and see if any letters have arrived. John Thomas!

    Enter Servant.

CORDER: Any, letters for X. Y. Z.?

SER: No, Sir, nor for A. B. C.

CORDER: Why did you not come when I rang half an hour ago?

SER: I was looking out of the window watching a man go by to execution.

    Slow music. CORDER *appears distraught.*

CORDER: Execution! What has he done?

SER: Oh, he'd been murdering some woman. Lor' bless me, Sir, you've got a face like a ghost!

CORDER: Leave the room.

SER: I'm off in the snapping of a pistol. (*Exit Ser.*)

    Faint strains of the Gipsy music. Servant returns.

CORDER: What's the matter now?

SER: There's a man below says he must see you.

CORDER: I don't feel in the humour to see visitors, tell the gentleman I'm not at home.

SER (*calls off*): Master says he's not at home.

CORDER: Oh, you blockhead!

SER: Oh, you blockhead!

CORDER: Get out. (*Kicks him out.*)

> *Enter* PHAROS LEE.

LEE: I beg pardon. Is your name William Corder?

CORDER: Yes, Sir, that is my name.

LEE: You formerly lived in Polestead, Suffolk?

CORDER: That is my native place, but I have not been there for some time.

LEE: Did you know a party there called Mathews?

CORDER: No, no, I know no one of that name.

LEE: Ayers, then?

CORDER: No, I cannot say I did.

LEE: You had an old Barn on your property called the Red Barn?

CORDER (*aside*): Who is this man? (*Aloud.*) Yes, quite true, Sir.

LEE: Did you ever know any one in Polestead called Maria Marten? (*Soft music.*)

CORDER: Oh, yes, Oh, yes, I knew the girl slightly. My brother introduced me at one of the village Merrymakings, when I was down from London.

LEE: Indeed! Is that all you know of her?

CORDER: What should I know more? And who are you, Sir, that questions me thus?

LEE: My name is Lee, I am a Bow Street Officer. Maria Marten has been murdered and her body found.

> *Gipsy music very loud.*

CORDER: But if her body has been found in the Red Barn what is this to do with me?

LEE: I did not say . . . *where* her body had been found.

CORDER: Oh, I have trapped myself, I understood —

LEE: And I understand you have partly confessed your crime, you are my prisoner.

CORDER: When was the body found?

LEE: On Friday last.

CORDER: The very morning of my dream.

LEE: I must search you, Sir.

He puts his hand in CORDER'S *pocket and finds a pistol.*

LEE: A pistol – loaded.

CORDER: Yes, I often take large sums of money to the Bank, it would not be safe to go unarmed.

LEE: 'Tis the fellow to the one found in the Red Barn. The same maker's name. William Corder, this is not the only crime you will have to answer to heaven for.

CORDER: What mean you?

He is answered by the Gipsy music.

LEE: Think of the poor gipsy you shot down.

CORDER: Ah, then you are . . .

LEE: The son of the man you murdered.

CORDER: Murdered?

LEE: Aye, murdered, you shot him down to seal his lips on some terrible secret he held of yours. That man you had wronged by betraying his child and driving her brother far away. I am that brother. On my father's grave I took the oath of vengeance to hunt you down. I joined the Law to complete my task. You are a prisoner within my hands, my vengeance is fulfilled.

CORDER: If you are my enemy, still you might do me one favour.

LEE: Anything within reason I will grant.

CORDER: As we pass along should you be questioned, will you say I am arrested for debt, not murder?

LEE: I will do so.

CORDER: The weather is cold, allow me to fetch my coat.

LEE: You can do so.

CORDER (*aside*): Thanks, by the window I may escape. (*Exit.*)

LEE: Ah, he would escape me! (*Rushes off.*)

Re-enters with WILLIAM.

LEE: Villain, I would have treated you like a gentleman, now I shall treat you as a common felon.

CORDER: Lost, lost!

CURTAIN

SCENE TWO

The wood.
Enter TIM *and* ANNE.

TIM: Come along, Anne! Dang it, we shall never get married.

ANNE: No, there's always summit in the way, who would have thought of our Maria being murdered! She should have waited till after we were married.

TIM: Aye, that she ought Nan, it were too bad of her, and after I'd bought a bright candlestick gold ring.

ANNE: Candlestick Gold, nay, nay, Gimlet Gold.

TIM: I went to Blacksmith for it. Says he, what's want a ring for? To get married says I. Get along says he, I only put rings thro' pigs' noses.

ANNE: Then did yer get ring?

TIM: Of course I did, I went to a jewellers' shop and asked him for a gold ring to get married with a big carbuncle on it.

ANNE: And has it got a carbuncle on it?

TIM: Nay, for the chap said it must be a plain to get married wi' and if I wanted a carbuncle I mun get it off parson's nose.

ANNE: Oh, Tim, do let us see it! My mouth waters to look at it. Oh, what a beauty, but it will be too big, Tim.

TIM: Then put it on thy thumb.

ANNE: Nay, nay, it will shrink up first wash day in wash tub.

TIM: Well, thee'st got ring so I go to Parsons and get married.

ANNE: Stop, stop, you cannot get married without me.

TIM: What, does it take two of us to get married?

ANNE: Of course, we go in Church two and come out one.

TIM: Well, dang my button's, how do they do that? Go in two and come out one, that's conjuring. Are we both rolled into one then? Blow the whiskers off the eyes of my Grandmother's sister's aunt's Tom Cat, if ever I heard of such a thing in all my life!

CURTAIN

SCENE THREE

A prison cell.
WILLIAM *discovered.*

CORDER: So ends my dream of wealth. Tried, condemned today to be executed, hundreds are flocking now to see me suspended between heaven and earth, the murderer's doom. Since my trial, night after night have I tried to sleep, but 'twas denied me. But now, when sleep eternal rapidly approaches in the form of death, my eyes grow weary, my eyelids close on the world of misery and thought.

His head drops, he falls asleep. MARIA *appears.*

MARIA: William, look on the murdered form of the girl who loved you, the last dread act of justice is about to be dealt upon thee. You thought to escape its power but the all-seeing eye was on your every actions. Farewell, I shall be near thee on the scaffold. (*Exit.* CORDER *starts up.*)

CORDER: Away, away, I dare not gaze upon that ghastly form, 'tis gone, a dream! How terrible! My brain reels, my flesh it quivers, and my heart it throbs to bursting.

> Such undistinguished horrors make my brain
> Like Hell the seat of darkness and of pain.

Enter PHAROS LEE.

LEE: Prisoner, the hour of your execution is at hand but an old man wishes to speak with you.

CORDER: Who is it?

LEE: The father of your victim, George Marten.

CORDER: I will not see him, yet stay (*aside*) the world would brand me coward, (*aloud*) admit him. (*Exit* LEE.)

CORDER: Courage, courage, William, for all your nerve is wanted now.

Enter MISTER MARTEN.

MARTEN: William, think not I come to upbraid in your last moments, though it was a cruel act to ruin my poor child then murder her, but now you are about to take the long journey into the valley of death a doubt is on my mind. Tell me, tell me truly, did you kill my poor child?

CORDER: No, no, I swear it is circumstantial evidence they have convicted me on, I am innocent, innocent.

MARTEN: Then heaven have mercy on them that condemn you. But be you innocent or guilty I came not to triumph, I pity and forgive you.

CORDER: Pity and forgiveness from you!

MARTEN: Yes, William, we all hope to be forgiven, so I repeat I forgive you and may heaven forgive you too.

CORDER: Mister Marten, your words have touched my heart, I will confess to you what I denied to my judge. I am guilty. Yes, I did kill Maria, but I have known no rest from that moment. I have suffered a thousand years of agony. Nightly the murdered spirit of Maria appears before me calling down heaven's justice. But now as I slept I thought she came to me, not as I last saw her in death at my feet but in all her radiant beauty. It was our marriage day, the bells rang out, we entered the Church and the words of the good priest were spoken. I was about to place the ring upon her hand when it fell from my grasp upon the marble pavement and shattered in a thousand pieces. I stooped to gather them, when the stones rolled back amidst a crash of thunder and there below I saw horrid demons and loathsome serpents sporting fearfully midst burning flames. I looked at Maria, a change had come, the fair flesh had fallen from her body and there I saw a ghastly skeleton. Her eyes shot sparks of fire, her hands had changed to eagle's claws, and seized my throat. She bore me down, down, yelling 'Welcome, murderer, to thy future home!' Oh, torture horrible!

> When Murder stains a soul with fearful dye,
> Then blood for blood is nature's dreadful cry.

He drops into a chair.

MARTEN: William, William, I would not have your conscience for all the gold the world would give. Repent, repent, ere it be too late! Farewell, William, and heaven have mercy on your soul! Oh, my poor child!

CORDER: Farewell, bless you for your forgiveness. Still from the scaffold I will proclaim – (*The Ghost of* MARIA *appears*) – Guilty!!!

He falls in a dead faint.

CURTAIN

SCENE FOUR

A street.
Enter NAN *and* TIM *crying.*

ANNE: Tim, Tim, isn't it dreadful!

TIM: Eas, it's awful, I cried all the water out of my eyes. Lend us that onion I seed thee with.

ANNE: What onion, Tim?

TIM: The one I saw you putting in your handkerchief to make you cry with.

ANNE: Get on thee fule, I can cry enough wi'out onions. I've cried so much till if I go on much more, I will cry myself away.

TIM: So here we are at Bury St. Edmunds come to see William Corders hung.

ANNE: Corders, Corder you mean. Shouldn't I like to pull his legs for killing our Maria and stopping us getting married.

TIM: Eas, and so would I, for he owes I ninepence. Dang me if I won't stop the execution and try and get my ninepence.

Enter OFFICER.

OFF (*to* TIM): How old are you?

TIM: What's that to thee?

OFF: How old are you?

TIM: About as old as my tongue and a bit older than my teeth. (OFFICER *measures him.*)

ANNE: Oh, Tim, he's a tailor and measuring you for a new suit for our marriage.

TIM: I say, what's up to?

OFF: You're very like . . .

TIM: Like what?

OFF: An escaped convict. I shall keep my eye on you. (*Exit* OFFICER.)

TIM: You better not or I shall knock it out.

ANNE: Did'st ever hear such a chap?

TIM: Come on or we shall be late to see the fun of William being hung.

ANNE: Fun, how can you say so, Tim!

TIM: Well, I want my ninepence and dang me if I won't have it.
Come on, Nan, dang me, but I'll have my ninepence. (*Both
exit.*)

CURTAIN

SCENE FIVE

The scaffold. CORDER *on the platform, a great crowd jostling at the
foot. Characters all on.* CORDER *steps forward and holds up his
hand; silence.*

CORDER: Be warned ye youths who see my sad despair,
   Avoid lewd women false as they are fair!
   By my example learn to shun my fate,
   How wretched is the man who's wise too late.

 Tremolo fiddles. The ghost of MARIA *appears on the scaffold.*
CORDER *shrieks.*
 Enter TIM, *pushing his way through the crowd.*
TIM: I want my ninepence, I want my ninepence.

CURTAIN